# ISLANDS & ATOLLS

LUIS CALLEJAS    LCLA OFFICE

PRINCETON ARCHITECTURAL PRESS, NEW YORK

PAMPHLET ARCHITECTURE 33

Published by
Princeton Architectural Press
37 East Seventh Street
New York, New York 10003

Visit our website at www.papress.com.

**ART WORKS.**
arts.gov

This project is supported in part by an award from the
National Endowment for the Arts.

Editor: Meredith Baber
Designer: Melissa Naranjo and Lukas Pauer / LCLA Office

Special thanks to: Sara Bader, Nicola Bednarek Brower, Janet Behning, Fannie Bushin,
Megan Carey, Carina Cha, Andrea Chlad, Barbara Darko, Benjamin English, Russell
Fernandez, Will Foster, Jan Hartman, Jan Haux, Emily Johnston-O'Neill, Diane Levinson,
Jennifer Lippert, Katharine Myers, Lauren Palmer, Margaret Rogalski, Dan Simon, Andrew
Stepanian, Elana Schlenker, Rob Shaeffer, Sara Stemen, Paul Wagner, and Joseph Weston of
Princeton Architectural Press —Kevin C. Lippert, publisher

Library of Congress Cataloging-in-Publication Data
Callejas, Luis, 1981–
 Pamphlet architecture 33 : islands & atolls / LCLA Office, Luis Callejas. — First [edition].
    pages cm. — (Pamphlet architecture ; 33)
 ISBN 978-1-61689-142-8 (pbk.)
 1. Callejas, Luis, 1981— Themes, motives. I. Title. II. Title: Islands & atolls.
 NA879.C35A4 2013
 724'.7--dc23
                        2013008611

HYDRIC

WEIGHTLESS

ATMOSPHERES

# Introduction

## Or a Project for Reclaiming an Archipelago

### Luis Callejas

▲

Luis Callejas (1981, Medellín, Colombia) is the Founding Director at LCLA Office, former founder of Paisajes Emergentes, and Lecturer at the Harvard Graduate School of Design.

Several months ago the Nicaraguan government presented an official complaint to the Hague International Court in the Netherlands asking to revisit dialogues from the seventies and eighties, to reclaim parts of the San Andrés archipelago, which are considered Colombian territories. The demand was partly agreed on and will transfer the sovereignty of 280,000 square kilometers of Colombian territorial waters to Nicaragua. In the judgment ruling of late 2012, the coralline formations of Serrana and Quita Sueño Banks will remain under Colombian control with a minuscule perimeter of territorial waters, and are now separated from the rest of the Colombian San Andrés Archipelago by Nicaraguan waters.

The reef formations are part of the San Andrés and Providencia Archipelago. The islands on the Colombian side have a population of about sixty thousand inhabitants, while the disputed coralline formations are unoccupied. They were formerly isolated and poorly known, but in the last decades they have become a regular stop on the Caribbean cruise ship circuit. Nicaragua formerly claimed the complete archipelago as well, but surrendered its claims in 1928 in return for Colombia's recognition of Nicaragua's sovereignty over the Islas del Maíz and the Mosquito Coast of the mainland. Later Nicaragua attempted to renounce this agreement, but in 2007 the International Court of Justice upheld the 1928 treaty establishing Colombian sovereignty. The court is continuing to consider the question of the maritime border between Nicaragua and Colombia, and in the meantime Nicaragua is continuing its claims to various uninhabited islands including the Serrana, Quita Sueño, and Roncador Banks.

Before the decision of 2012, the most recent treaty between Colombia and the United States—which occupied Nicaragua at the time—dated from 1972 and 1981 and gave the U.S. the fishing rights and resource exploitation in the waters surrounding the disputed unoccupied atolls and reefs. It was decided that no country could claim the "islands" as they had been permanently below sea level and were only temporarily exposed during low tides, and thus are not considered islands according to international law of the sea. In exchange Colombia received the sovereignty of a lighthouse located in the Quita Sueño reef, as well as the navigation beacon towers in Serrana and Roncador. In short, this strange turn essentially gave the water rights to the U.S. and sovereignty on all artificial structures to Colombia.

The Serrana and Quita Sueño Banks where the structures are located are former atolls, now primarily submerged platforms consisting of shallow reef environments. The structures, dating from 1977, are square skeletal towers painted with red and white horizontal bands and mounted on a square platform supported by piles.

The Serrana Bank is about 360 kilometers east of Nicaragua. The U.S. renounced its claim to the Serrana and Quita Sueño Banks in 1981, but both are still claimed by Nicaragua.

The Quita Sueño Bank is about 40 kilometers long and 32 kilometers wide, covering an area of over 1,200 square kilometers, almost entirely under water. Three small cays and two rocks emerge above the water to form the bank's islands. They are largely barren, with sparse vegetation of bushes and some trees. Quita Sueño is about 110 kilometers northeast of Providencia Island and 70 kilometers west of the Serrana Bank; the reef is entirely submerged for most of the year. A 2010 Colombian postage stamp shows both Quita Sueño lighthouses, but Google satellite view does not show the reef at all.

In launching their complaint to the tribunal, Nicaragua rejected the previous agreement between Colombia and the U.S., stating that since the treaties were ratified when the U.S. occupied Nicaragua, they were no longer applicable. In 2002, before receiving the decision of the international court, Nicaragua launched a competition for oil exploration aimed at U.S. and European big oil companies. Now that the water is assigned to Nicaragua, it is very likely that the Colombian partly-submerged territories will become the only protected ecology of the Archipelago.

How can the smallest possible entities— not even land, but structures ceded by the U.S. to Colombia as remnants of a lost legal battle—become the most powerful tools for reclaiming sovereignty over an oceanic archipelago?

How could a series of tactical interventions to the lighthouses and navigation beacons become the key elements to protecting the ecologies of the Archipelago, and finally trigger an understanding of it as an oceanic territory of a country?

There are no inhabitants of the islands and atolls that are now located within Nicaraguan waters; however, the territories are daily occupied by Colombian fishermen who travel from local settlements. How can small-scale interventions to the structures change the cultural perception of the seemingly unoccupied landscapes that so many fishermen depend on?

The projects contained in *Islands & Atolls* are a collection of works that share these questions. In all the projects there is an interest in how architecture might critically repurpose its traditionally limited disciplinary tools to have an impact at a territorial scale and ultimately instigate how the territorial effects might be categorized by appropriating the term *landscape*. This collection of works is not the production of a true landscape architecture studio, but rather the investigations of an intense interest in territorial and hinterland issues tackled through the disciplinary tool of a Latin American architecture practice. In the case of Colombia—where landscape architecture does not really exist as an established field—it becomes a true hybrid form of operations. It is a practice in which a deep understanding of territorial politics, and aquatic resources, designed atmospheres, and an expanded notion of environment are driving forces to generate future landscapes.

▲ CF. 6

▲ CF. 6

fig. 1 Serrana
(Stamp from 1956)

fig. 2 Quitasueño
(Stamp from 2010)

Traditionally, strategies for claiming sovereignty of oceanic territories have been through oil exploration or a military presence. The Quita Sueño lighthouse will house a Colombian oceanic research station. Controlled fishing outside the atoll and a totally protected landscape in the interior will be the soft tactic for reclaiming the reef. In ten years, when Colombia will be able to present the case again to the tribunal, it will be possible to prove the extended urbanization of the reef and its close relationship with the rest of the Colombian Archipelago.

Tactic A: The reef as protected landscape

Ironically, the reef formations that support the structures could not be categorized as islands as part of the Archipelago, because they are submerged for most of the year. Now the structures have become sovereign islands within the Nicaraguan territory. As part of the series of tactics to reclaim the Archipelago, we propose the creation of a Nicaraguan embassy in the platform of the lighthouse tower. A political island within the minimum sovereign entity of Colombia, the new embassy will be able to support the efforts for safeguarding the oceanic region's stability.

Tactic B: An island within an island within an island: Project for a new Nicaraguan embassy

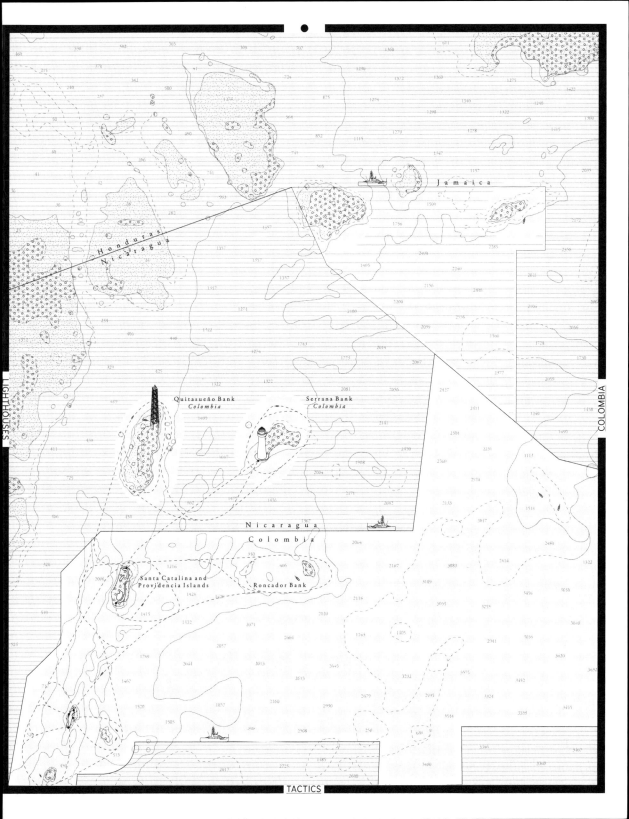

Honduras

Nicaragua

J a m a i c a

COLOMBIA

Quitasueño Bank
Colombia

Serrana Bank
Colombia

N i c a r a g u a

C o l o m b i a

Santa Catalina and
Providencia Islands

Roncador Bank

# TACTICAL ARCHIPELAGO

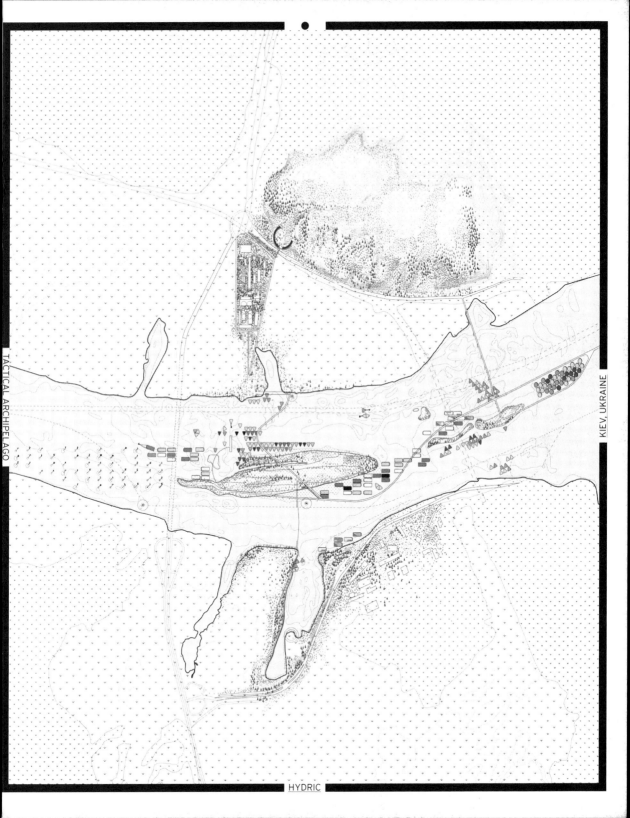

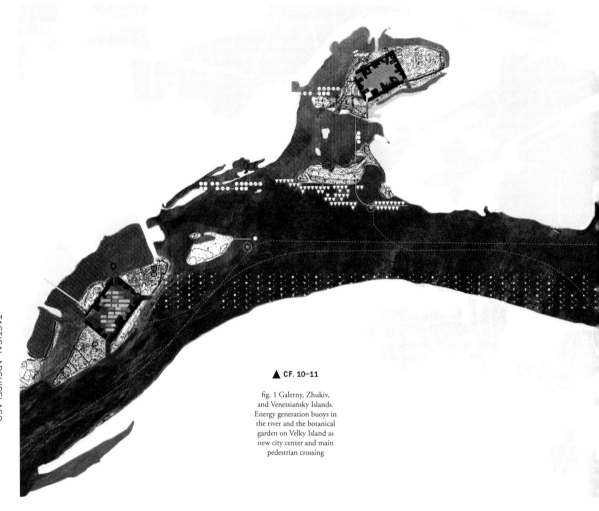

▲ CF. 10–11

fig. 1 Galerny, Zhukiv,
and Venetsiansky Islands.
Energy generation buoys in
the river and the botanical
garden on Velky Island as
new city center and main
pedestrian crossing

By reappropriating historic areas of preservation as vital city centers through small aquatic itinerant interventions, the project turns formerly isolated areas into ways to connect the shores of a wide river dividing the city of Kiev, Ukraine. Historically untouched as hunting reserves and areas to be preserved, an archipelago of thirty-seven islands in the Dnieper River serves as a unique ground of opportunity to rethink a city.

Varying in time of deployment and location, a series of micro-tactical interventions intend to recover forgotten and unfulfilled desires of the citizens of Kiev: taking a bath in

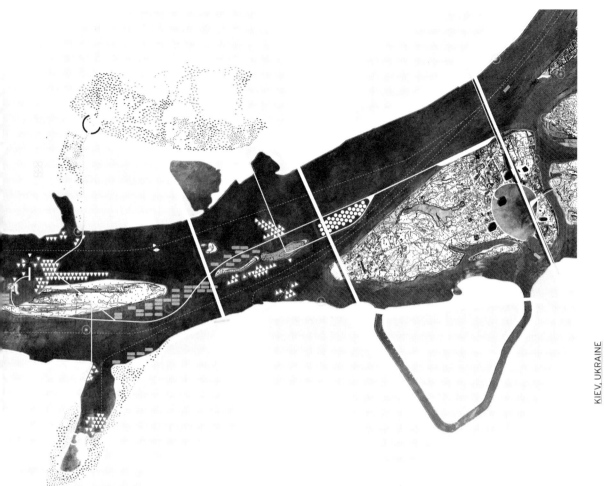

the river, taking a walk in the forest, or simply getting in touch with the seemingly pristine nature in proximity to the city's center. Specialized action clusters create a new relation with the linear geography, where a third zone is formed by transferring water to firm ground and vice versa, supported by new activities, new landscape references, preservation of delicate ecologies, allowing for new forms of collectivity and engagement with the river landscape.

Itinerant landscape units are deployed to amplify existing situations, introducing new ways of engagement with the landscape: inflatable art for the

○

▲ CF. 12–13

fig. 2 Underwater view of
the new botanical garden
on Velky Island. (The contamination
of the Dnieper River from the
Chernobyl disaster is just a myth.)

○

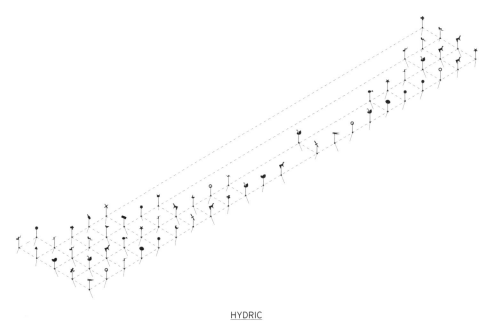

HYDRIC

ISLAND QUEEN

production of energy, garden barges, and floating infrastructures that could transform zones whenever needed. While North–South interventions preserve the islands in order to configure a selective landscape through soft urbanization tactics, East–West interventions connect specific sites such as the extension of a botanical garden with the city itself. In addition, Program Activity Bridges allow the infrastructure to have different services rather than act solely as crossing surfaces.

▲ **CF. 14, 15**

fig. 3 View of the energy generation buoys from the main bridge

fig. 4 Axonometric view of a curated event for inflatable art attached to energy generation buoys in the Dnieper River

x x x x x x x x x x

fig. 5 View from the artificial iceberg park during the ice fishing season

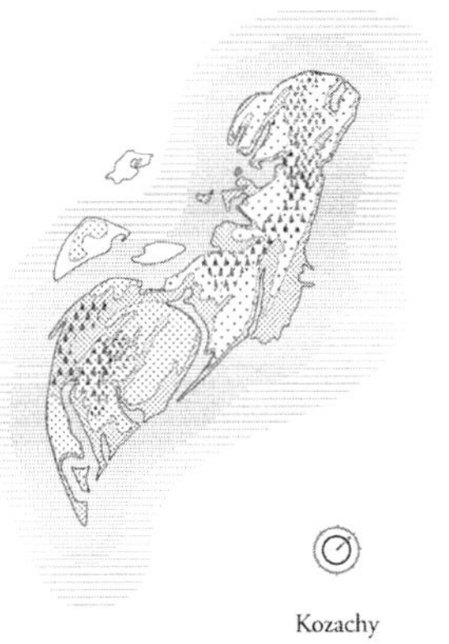

TACTICAL ARCHIPELAGO

Kozachy

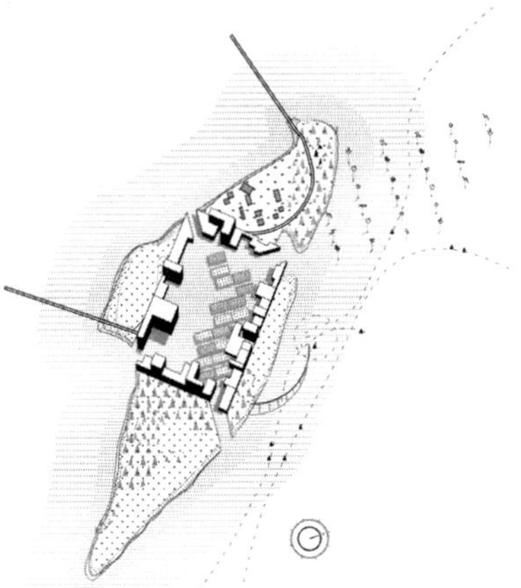

Zhukiv

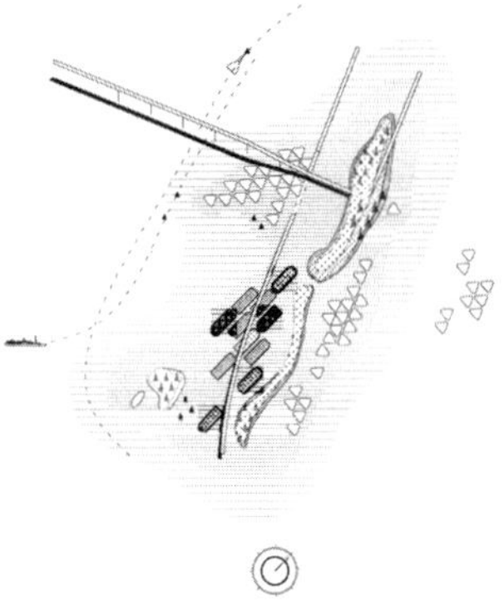

Kyiv Botanical Garden Islands

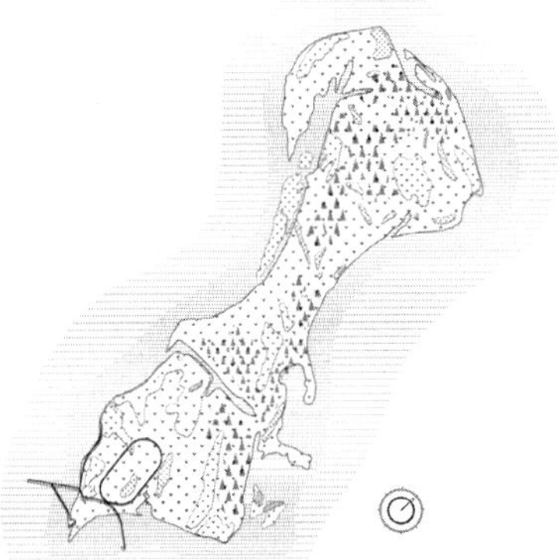

Muromets

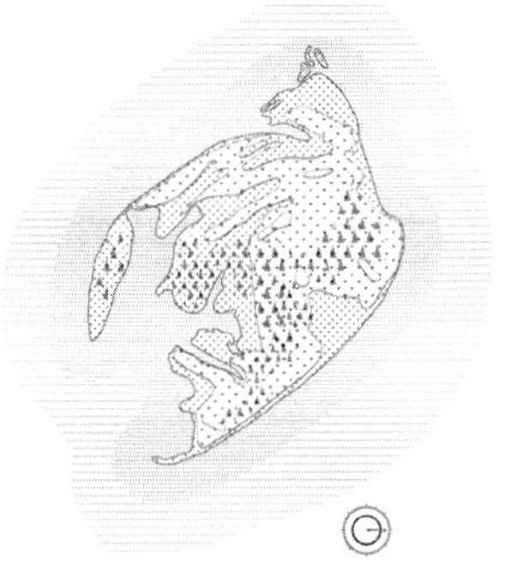

Olzhyn

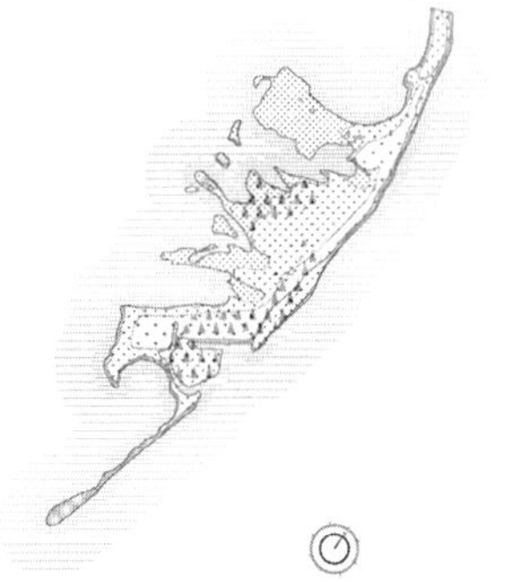

Vodnikov

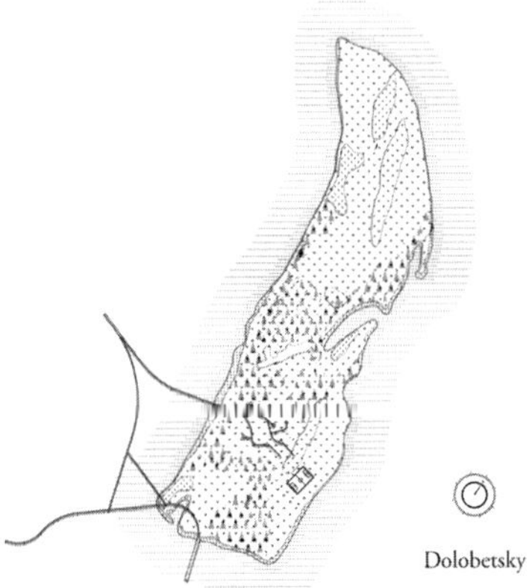

Dolobetsky

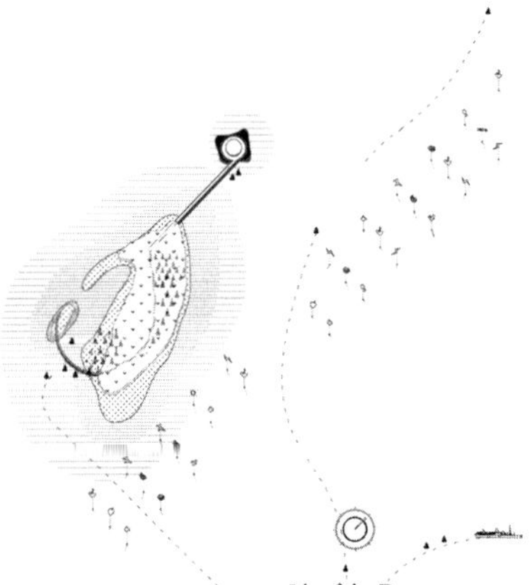

Isle of the Dogs

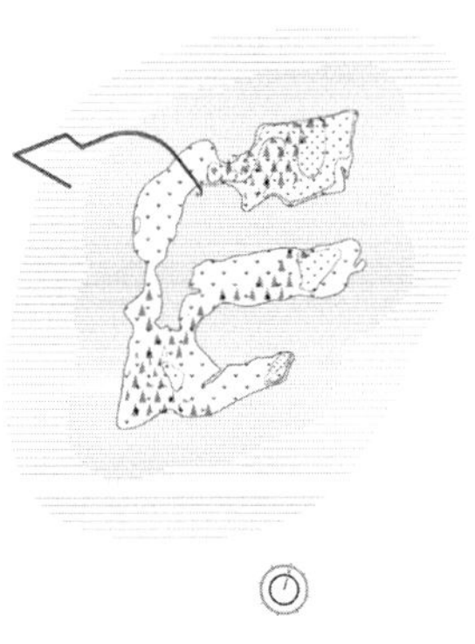

Lapuhovaty

HYDRIC

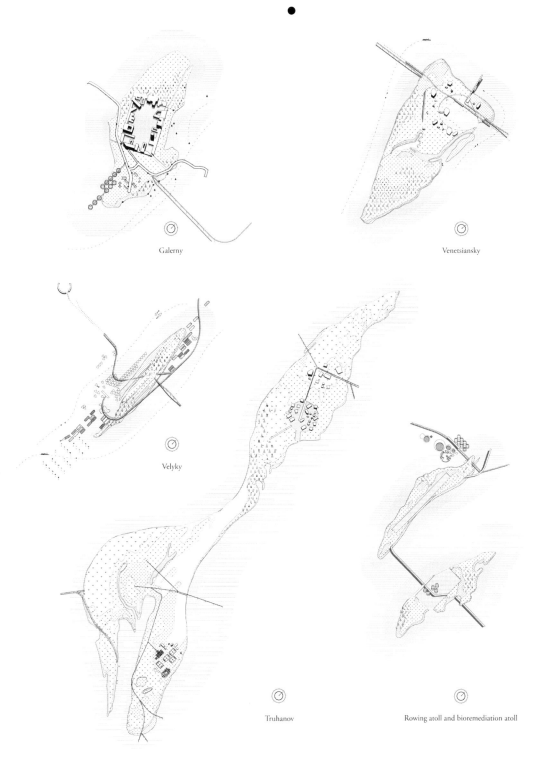

Galerny

Venetsiansky

Velyky

Truhanov

Rowing atoll and bioremediation atoll

HYDRIC

O

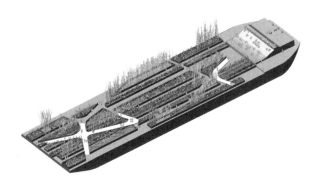

HYDRIC

▲ CF. 18

fig. 6 Floating
Soccer Field

fig. 7 Fragmented
Botanical Garden

fig. 8 Floating
Iceberg Park

▲ CF. 19

fig. 9 View of the interventions on
Venetsiansky, Dolobetsky, and
Truhanov Islands

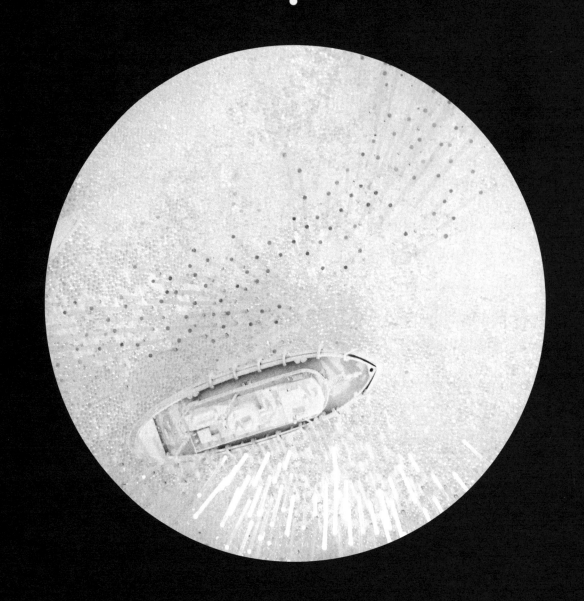

# VENICE LAGOON

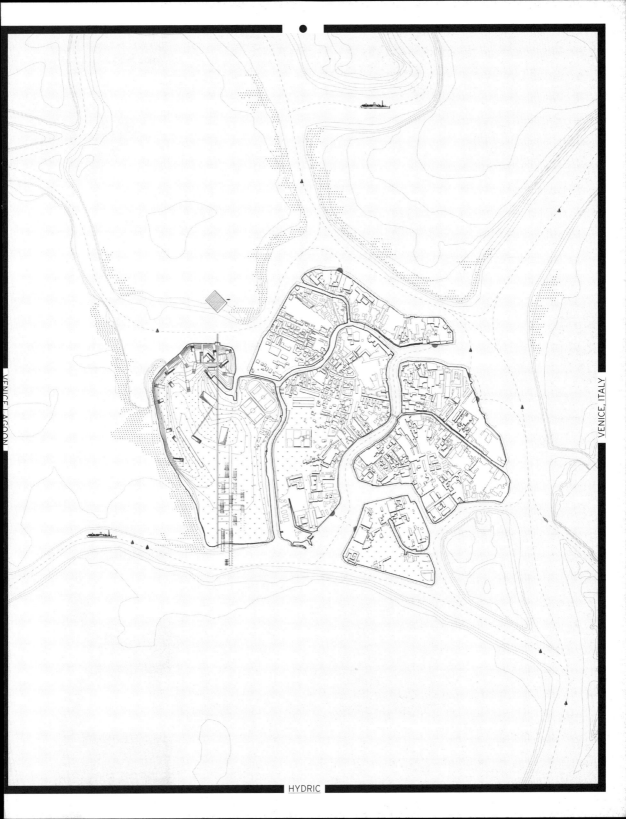

○

▲ CF. 22, 23

fig. 1 Section view across a
typical Venice block, where the
abandoned houses act as new
continuous public spaces.

fig. 2 Underwater view of
the artificial reef

× × × × × × × × × ×

fig. 3 Venetian Lagoon

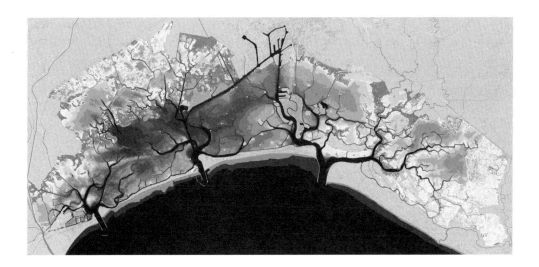

As a canonical case of aquatic urbanization, the Venice Lagoon in Italy is an ideal ground for tactical interventions that trigger new forms of public life tied to aquatic events. Varying in scope and scale, the project strategically intervenes at the building scale of decaying houses threatened with collapse, a tidal park at the vacant island of Sacca San Mattia, and at the territorial scale of an artificial reef to partly recover the lagoon's threatened ecology.

Removing the roofs but conserving the facades transforms residential buildings into open public spaces as they become abandoned or obsolete because of water damage. New gardens, galleries, small parks, and public baths appear behind their walls, eventually generating a decentralized system of dispersed yet connected micro-parks. As a means of forecasting future landscape and climate events, the uninhabited island of Sacca San Mattia becomes a testing ground for the amplification and replication of the almost invisible, slow drowning of Venice. Through its simple features such as canals and trenches, the paths of the new park on the island register tidal cycles, to the extent of becoming inaccessible during high tide. As territorial infrastructure, the artificial reef aims to protect and preserve weakened ecologies in the lagoon resulting from the constant traffic of the Vaporetto system of public ferries. Thus, the reef becomes both a highway for boats and a hotbed for the lagoon ecosystem, as it eventually disappears from view under the rising tides of the lagoon.

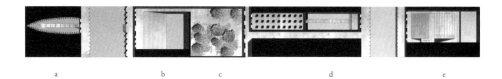

a                     b       c               d               e

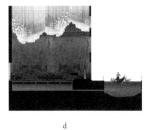

▲ **CF. 24**

fig. 4 Plan (top) and section (bottom) views across a series of interior spaces

× × × × × × × × × ×

fig. 5 The artificial reef acts as an aquatic highway for the Vaporetto system of public ferries.

d                                                e

a                          b                        c

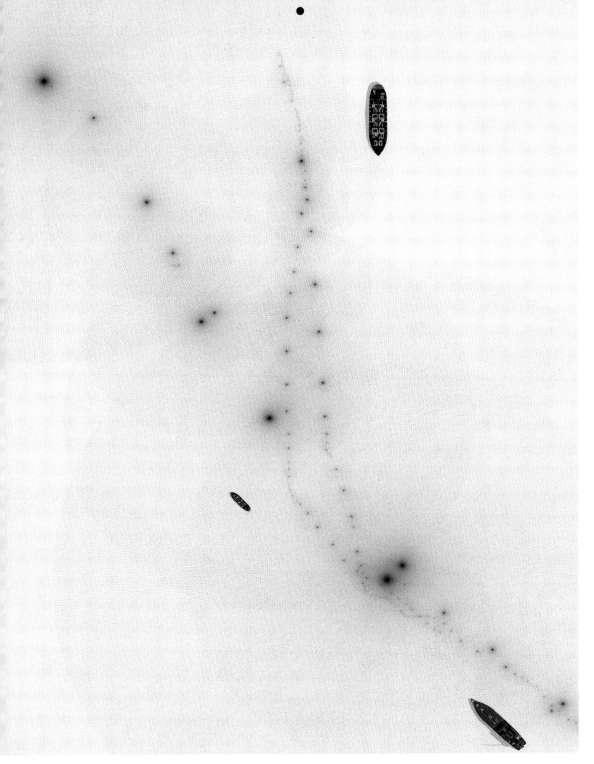

# RIO OLYMPIC
# PARK

HYDRIC

RIO DE JANEIRO, BRAZIL

HYDRIC

○

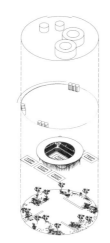

HYDRIC

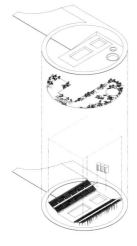

▲ **CF. 28, 29**

fig. 1 Exploded axonometric drawings of the different sport venues linked by the continuous platform

× × × × × × × × × ×

fig. 2. View of the tennis arena. Pedestrians can enjoy a free experience of the games from above.

Located on an artificial peninsula and former Formula 1 racing track in Rio de Janeiro, Brazil, the master plan for the Olympic Park becomes the ideal testing ground for a new model of an open-air sports complex in which its main programs are grouped in a compact vertical arrangement. As a result, the structures act as activity focal points that create new forms of engagement between visitors and the rich ecosystem of the Jacarepaguá Lagoon.

This model operates in a sectional logic as both the public areas and the service spaces of the facilities are organized in a stacked manner rather than separated in plan. Thus, rather than creating an iconographic building, one vital open-air scenario is generated. A large platform linking the various programs allows for pedestrians to have direct views of the games from a raised perspective. Traversing the typologies of a small city and a big park, the master plan serves as a fluid and open public platform for massive audiences.

▲ **CF. 30, 31**

fig. 3 Exploded axonometric drawing of the island exposing the stacking of programs and the future city

× × × × × × × × × ×

fig. 4 Plan view of the Jacarepaguá Lagoon showing its proximity to the Atlantic Ocean

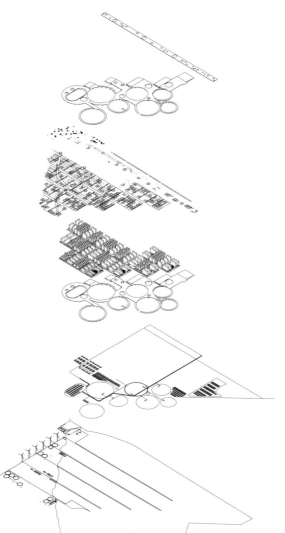

HYDRIC

# LAKE PARK

HYDRIC

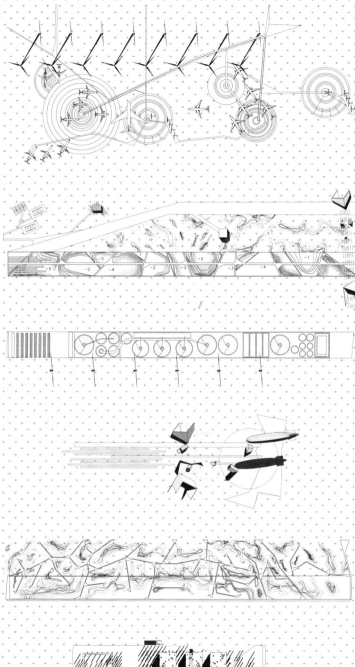

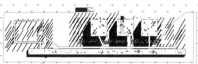

Situated in the metropolitan region of Quito, Ecuador, in the Andes mountain range, Mariscal Sucre International Airport is an obsolete airfield with a surface of 126 hectares. Through flooding the runway of the old airport, the project aims to generate an active hydrologic park. The transformation of the runway into an urban park is an opportunity to test the insertion of leisure activities and aquatic ecosystems typical to the tropics.

Serving as an impervious platform for a series of linked aquatic interventions, the 3,120-meter runway would be composed of outdoor rooms, designed to have a distinct programmatic character ranging from an open-air

aquarium to thermal baths, to be phased in over many years. Thus, the linear landscape of events can be understood as a giant hydric machine made up of smaller habitable parts. Forming a cycle of aquatic events, the runway is divided into six stages, while pedestrian walkways allow people to engage in natural processes that are typically foreign to urban environments.

The park is divided in six stages along the runway that act as a giant hydric machine. In the first stage, nine lakes work alternately to treat the residual water of the park and nearby buildings. An excavated open-air aquarium is then filled with partially processed water from the wetlands. This aquarium

▲ CF. 34, 35

fig. 1 View of the nine remediation lakes
and aquatic botanical garden

× × × × × × × × × ×

fig. 2 Thermal baths and pools in
the flooded runway

contains tropical fauna from fluvial ecosystems around the world. Next, water coming from the aquarium contains organic material that is ideal for maintaining the fertilization of an aquatic botanical garden with tropical species. With a conventional treatment plant, water coming from the botanical garden is oxygenated and filtrated while organic material is removed. In the next stage, clean water is used to fill public pools and thermal baths, while a combination of eolic and solar energy is used to heat the aquatic complex. Finally, through simple exposure to the sun, water is collected from a recreational lake and processed with chlorine and other substances that decontaminate water in subterranean tanks that can be used for irrigation systems and general park maintenance.

O

▲ **CF. 36, 37, 38–39**

fig. 3 Exploded view of the six
hydric components that align with
the old runway: the lake, the
pools, the treatment plant, the
botanical garden, the aquarium,
and the remediation wetlands

× × × × × × × × ×

fig. 4  Plan view of Lake Park with
the open-air aviation museum in the
center and the complete series of
aligned aquatic events distributed
along the runway

× × × × × × × × ×

fig. 5 Model of the open-air
aviation museum

HYDRIC

## Luis Callejas in conversation with Mason White

▲ OCT 10, 2012

Mason White is Partner at Lateral Office in Toronto, Canada. L. Callejas and M. White have collaborated on projects like Weatherfield on the Persian Gulf or Peaks and Valleys on the Faroe Islands. In spring 2012 they taught a studio together at the University of Toronto.

MW: I was thinking we could start not with your work but in the context I see some of your work coming out of, which is of course where you were raised: Medellín, Colombia, and the Andes. Especially the topography of those places, the varying degrees of atmosphere, and the relationship between extreme urbanism and extreme landscape—"the wild," in a way, informs your work.

LC: [laughs] I was not raised in "the wild." But yes, there are blurry limits between urbanism, landscape, and architecture down there.

MW: To be very personal about it, I have been there with you. It was an amazing two weeks. I had the opportunity to meet your father and see the place in which he works and his paintings, and I was really struck by a tension between your father's work as an artist and your continuity with that as a form of expression, but at a more territorial scale. I see your father was already working at an intimate, almost biological scale, and then I see you in some ways continuing—like all influences in some ways— your father's interest in landscape painting. I wonder if you might talk about those connections.

LC: The first time I heard about "landscape" was because of my parents, not because of my education as an architect. Both my father and my mother were landscape artists. My mother was an architect, too—born and educated in Caracas, Venezuela— and she used to work at the Caracas Botanical Garden doing botanical illustrations. At the same time, my father was in Colombia, doing mostly radical landscape painting. My strongest memories are from when I was between six and eleven years old, when my father started to include my toy robots and airplanes as the main theme of his paintings. This was between the eighties and nineties, when he started to work in a series called Paisajes Agredidos. He became recognized for going beyond picturesque images of the Andean landscape. He started to include objects of war, most notably with shadows of airplanes and MiG-29 fighter jets above the grass and close-ups of grass blown by the wind. I think he was not really that interested in war as landscape, but more in the effect of those highly technological objects in the landscape—almost like animals in the fields. He started this series by working with graphics from the airplane magazines he used to buy for me. He would then

call me to help him name the paintings.

MW: When we went to your father's studio, there was a study on the wall of a particular plant—this amazing leaf. Can you describe it?

LC: Yes, it is called Yarumo. It turns silver in color only between a confined altitude range above sea level. When aviation started in Colombia, the pilots would use those silver-colored trees to help determine their altitude.

MW: Wasn't your first job actually in a botanical garden? In a way what was happening within your domestic life seems to have manifested itself in your career. How did you end up there?

LC: Yes, I became interested in landscape at the midpoint of my architectural education. I think the truth is that I was more interested in the nonbuilt environment around Medellín than its architectural heritage. I never got interested in these boring brick buildings. I decided to work on the botanical garden for my design thesis, which caught the attention of the director and they immediately hired me; they were starting to renovate the facilities. Interestingly, because I was not a landscape architect, they gave us an office shared with the botanist and biologists in order to collaborate in the renovation—that was between 2005 and 2007.

MW: From there you were working with Paisajes Emergentes. You knew Sebastian Mejia and Edgar Mazo from school, and they were all pursuing

Emergentes was, in a way, driven by positive skepticism: by their need to perceive landscape as a technical device—drawn in the same terms of architecture—and my need to adapt their architectural propositions to fit in open-ended and usually wild environments.

of something airborne, something that defies gravity. I feel as though they are related, but I think it is too convenient to suddenly relate them. First we have to talk about air, and then we have to talk about horizontality. Were you a kite enthusiast when you were young?

LC: Yes, I was specifically interested in kites.

different work. The collaboration started just after you finished working at the botanical garden. Did your role in the practice become that of the landscape by default?

LC: They were extremely interested in landscape, too. But they had a completely different approach, as they came from working in a really good architecture practice. I think the production of Paisajes

MW: Collaborative work always ends up with someone convincing the other. Lola [Sheppard] and I do the same. But I think we should talk more about this fascination you have with buoyancy, lightness, and weightlessness. To put it very simply, it feels like there are two projects that you are very interested in: horizontal islands—pools and landscape rooms— and a vertical, almost two-dimensional project

MW: Is it that easy to say? Is this the fascination? Maybe it's the beginning of it?

LC: Airplanes fascinate me, and kites were an obvious way to turn that into something real. The same thing usually happens for architects. We don't design airplanes; our production is clunky and primitive next to airplanes, but we can flirt with kite and balloon design. The

▲ CF. 41

fig. 1 MiG-29 (1988), Rodrigo Callejas, acrylic on canvas, 100 x 80 cm, Medellín, Colombia

Cloud project in Ituango was a commission for a high-rise structure that triggered a series of projects in our studio rooted in a childlike fascination. We needed the height, and that was something we never thought that we would do. The commission came at a time when we were interested in horizontal surfaces and water. The ultralight and airborne objects started as a reaction to the fact that it was strange for a landscape-oriented practice to receive a commission for a tall vertical structure.

MW: And the ephemerality of the balloons, under constant threat of being erased, right? In that way they are like islands under threat of reclamation by the surrounding environment.

LC: Yes, and also in this case the need for height was pragmatic. The client wanted us to design a communication antenna, and they needed it to be high because the topography is so varied in the Andes, otherwise the communication between the five towns would be interrupted. We became interested in achieving really high altitudes through simple procedures and new ways of locating radio antennas. After that we did the same for Surrey—which is flat.

MW: But they also wanted a vertical element?

LC: Not really. That time we were interested in doing a tall yet weightless tower: a fake skyscraper.

MW: But then came Airplot, which is almost a demonstration. In that project you are using balloons to prevent flights. And that project was also a competition, not a commission. What was the brief?

LC: The brief was very simple: Greenpeace bought a small plot located on the site of the future third runway for London Heathrow Airport. The competition called for a structure strong enough to make the construction of a third runway impossible. They wanted a barricade, so we proposed an airborne one, not to stop the construction but to disrupt air traffic.

MW: Do you see these aerial projects as landscapes, architecture, or art? How do you define an inflatable house floating above a real house?

LC: I wouldn't know exactly, that was just an aerial barricade....To which field do barricades belong? It would fit in engineering and infrastructure as well.

MW: Do you see these as islands as well?

LC: Yes, they contain specific interests that deal with expanded fields. They are islands because the boundaries are always hard and well defined.

MW: You have also done more traditional landscape proposals, such as the Quito project. This returns us to the project of extreme horizontality, which is distinguished from these aerial landscapes.

LC: Yes, but even in that large-scale park, it is about compartments. Sometimes we care about ecology as medium, but always contained. There is nothing wrong with contained ecologies and hard boundaries.

MW: There is not a tradition in landscape architecture to treat landscape as rooms. Rooms are usually understood as enclosed gardens. I think the island is an interesting device in which to make a room-sized landscape. Because the island is small, by nature it has an intimate, almost domestic quality to it: smallness by which you can create radical difference. In the Kiev project you were exploring the idea that along the river bank you would end up with a zoo of possibilities. Literally all the islands operate as landscape species, or possible hybrids of water urbanism and islandness.

LC: Yes, but still, those radical differences occur at the interior, and those islands in the Kiev project are almost always the size of a big building. So if we focus on techniques and scale, the rooms are gardens, islands, and buildings at the same time.

MW: They are architecturalized—artificial ecologies in a way that a city is understood to be as well.

LC: We came really late to Ungers. Which in a way is good. He didn't care much about the space in between the islands.

MW: I think that the fascination with the term *archipelago* or even the possibility of it as a territory in Ungers is much more architecture and urban-centric. So it is interesting that in a way, although you made reference to Ungers, I think you are much more innovative with adapting archipelagos literally as a sort of living dynamic site, whereas I see others borrowing the Ungers concept and applying it metaphorically to the concept of the city. It is interesting that you have brought the archipelago back to its origin. It is the

space between Greece and Turkey: the four thousand little islands in the Aegean Sea. It is not an urban idea, but actually a kind of very threatening territory.

LC: That threatening or wild aquatic geography is usually more interesting than the islands. That is why it is not about monuments but about landscapes that are contained and controlled and heavily designed. They behave as platforms to enjoy the vast space that separates them.

MW: I have seen you present your work, and although we are having a very serious conversation, I think there is a sense of humor in your projects. For example, the synchronized swimmers in your pools project with the window, and this idea that the construction workers would witness it and it became a kind of attraction to them...Or the idea of the balloon copies of houses. Is it fair to say that you are injecting humor; or do you admit to the possibility for architecture to be fantastic, where one sees a project and laughs?

LC: Sometimes it is really direct, like the stadium competition that we won in Bogotá. It was a competition for the main soccer stadium, and we decided to camouflage the building instead of adding

a new facade. For us it was more ridiculous to add a new facade to that ugly 1930s monster that has already been through six renovations.

MW: But why? Do you think architecture is too serious?

LC: Yes, I do. In the pools project we were having fun imagining people stalking the swimmers, but then we won and it was built. It became proof that these situations are the ones that create the biggest moments of engagement among the public and the building. Actually, those windows are really ugly because that pool should have been buried. All the guts and pipes are exposed, but people don't care and just want to stalk the swimmers. Keep in mind that it was done in Medellín, and those windows look out to what is supposed to be public space. Something like that would never have happened in that context before.

MW: Well, I am sympathetic to the idea that architecture is too serious. In a way I think you enjoy the ridiculous.

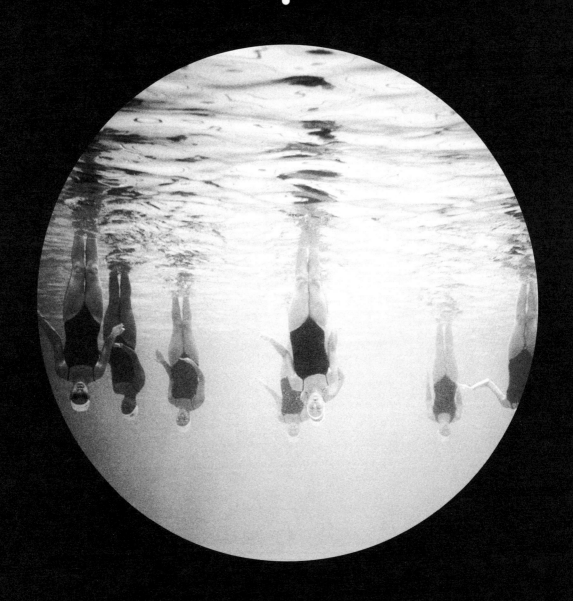

# FLOODINGS

fig. 1 Model of the Airplot project—
a demonstration to stop air traffic

fig. 2 Open-air aquariums as part of the
riverfront park in Temuco, Chile

fig. 3 Model of a prototype for the Venice Lagoon—
an inverted ship inside an abandoned house

fig. 4 Model of the exhibition space
in Mexico City, August 2011

fig. 5 Model of a prototype for the Venetian
Lagoon—a flooded theater inside a house

fig. 6 Underwater view of the synchronized
swimming pool in Medellín, Colombia

fig. 7 Models of the prototypes for the Venice
Lagoon inside abandoned houses

fig. 8 Passersby peeking at the synchronized
swimmers from the inner street

fig. 9 Confined gardens inside
one of the houses in Venice

FLOODINGS

fig. 10 View from the gallery at 7 pm when heavy condensation starts to form on the glass

fig. 11 Airplot, Aquariums, and the Venice Lagoon prototypes displayed on a hydrogel bed

fig. 12 Lake Park project in Quito, view of the open-air aviation museum model and the flooded runway

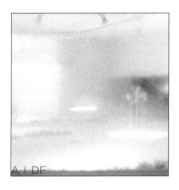

fig. 13 View from the exterior of the gallery when the interior cloud forms

fig. 14 There is space for only one person inside the gallery. The main views are from outside

▲ CF. 46–47

Images of the exhibition at LIGA, space for architecture in Mexico City, August 2011

fig. 15 The artificial reef emerges out of the hydrogel bed. When the gel dries up, the reef is exposed.

fig. 16 Lamps located below the table heat up the hydrogel bed to create the cloud

fig. 17 150 liters of water flood the table, solidifying on contact with the hydrogel

LIGA 02

*Floodings* is an installation in which a gallery space becomes a temporary flooded garden to exhibit five projects designed for and situated in five different cities. Although each one responds to a specific geographic context with dissimilar conditions, the cities share a series of extreme hydrological phenomena.

▲ **CF. 48–49**

fig. 18 Night photograph from Avenida Insurgentes. When the gallery closes, an artificial cloud starts to form, lasting until the gallery is open again the next morning.

The exhibition subtly modifies atmospheres and environments inside the gallery as visitors arrive. A high temperature and humid environment is generated as the gallery is "flooded" with water retained in hydrogel—minuscule spherical polymer particles mostly used in agriculture, greenhouses, and hydroponic farming, able to absorb up to 150 times their own weight in water. The punctual lighting from below illuminates the exhibited models and simultaneously heats up the hydrogel, forcing the water to evaporate, and thus creating an artificial interior cloud in almost total humidity inside the gallery. As a result, the gallery windows are cloudy whenever the gallery is closed, yet passersby can still observe the conditions from the exterior.

# Luis Callejas
# in conversation with
# Geoff Manaugh

▲ JAN 10, 2013

Geoff Manaugh founded
the architecture blog
BLDGBLOG and is the
Director of Studio-X
at the Columbia Graduate
School of Architecture,
Planning and Preservation
in New York City.

GM: Islands are often seen as utopian spaces standing apart from the very world they aim to update or perfect. Thomas More's *Utopia* literally was an island, for instance. However, this sense of divergence or separation from the rest of the human community has also been taken up by dystopian science fiction visions, from *The Island of Dr. Moreau* to the blockbuster *The Island*. However, islands are also well known as evolutionary hotbeds, hosting incredible species that emerge, thrive, interbreed, and speciate yet further. The most obvious example of this is Charles Darwin's Galapagos. Could you perhaps discuss the role of utopian isolation in your work?

LC: Embracing isolation as a desirable condition allows me to produce in a way in which I have a high control over the limits of interventions while maintaining the opportunity for unexpected results within those limits. As a method, it liberates my work from some of the contemporary moral weights assigned to ecology as a design medium. I am interested in designed ecologies, but at the same time, it is frustrating when design vitality is forced to step back just because of the infinitely interconnected implications of dealing with live matter. Recently—and much too late—generative-based

approaches to design have become relevant in the field of landscape architecture, partly to deal with that moral weight. I am not interested in that at all but rather need the recognizable boundaries. My work is situated on the boundary between architecture and landscape—it is often territorial, yet I am not interested in open-ended indeterminacy or endless process-based repetition.

GM: What about isolation's effects in terms of evolutionary change or adaptation? I'm also curious if the unpredictability of evolution also challenges your design practice.

LC: Isolating ecologies as a means to trigger unexpected reactions—not necessarily positive ones—is fascinating to me. In this, your reference to Dr. Moreau is an appropriate association; he is a designer, and as such he is open to failure, while Darwin is merely an observer. Moreau needed the island as a container of his work. In a way it is about the potentials of quarantine and not really evolution. Going back to the geographic categories, I think the atoll is a better term to frame my interest in contained unpredictability. I like the determinacy of the external figure—the figure defined by the beach is clear, yet it is vulnerable to erosion and wear. At the same time the liquid interior gives me a perfect

frame for vital and amoral play with live matter as a design medium.

GM: In an era of rising sea levels and shrinking glaciers, the "island" seems to be an increasingly omnipresent category—as if islands were really the secret logic of terrain everywhere. Whole new islands, for instance, have been "discovered" off the coast of Greenland as the ice cap melts: what once appeared to be peninsulas are revealed as islands after the ice has disappeared. The island was there all along, we could say; it was simply hidden. In any case, could you address the idea that islands are, in fact, hidden in plain sight all around us, and how the idea of the emergent island—or an island yet to appear—is a more common landform in today's geography?

LC: Geographers distinguish two kinds of islands: oceanic—ancient isolated landmasses; and continental—fragments derived from continental masses. Thus all emerging or yet to appear non-volcanic islands are of the continental type. They will likely form new archipelagos and very rarely be completely isolated. In a world of urbanized coasts it can mean two things: urban islands or total disaster, or possibly both.

GM: Do you see potentials for your practice here?

LC: In a way, these hidden or emerging islands are future fragments of past continents. Some of them are the size of buildings, while others are the size of cities or parks. It is fascinating to think of the potentials of occupying those new landforms that derive from larger territories. The formation of these new archipelagos is not necessarily restricted to the effects of global warming. My work deals with processes of urbanization on those yet-to-appear platforms, in all scales, from temporary research stations on top of floating ice to parks occupying newly isolated land in extreme landscapes.

GM: The construction of artificial islands is seemingly as old as human beings themselves. The first artificial islands are not in Dubai, of course. Prehistoric island-building projects from South America, where islands are more like textiles woven together by reeds, and even Neolithic Ireland, where manufactured island-structures called *crannogs* were used as housing, show how old the practice is. The list could go on and on. In this era of rapid mechanical dredging and other crossover technologies from marine construction, where might island construction go next?

LC: The future is not as much about the territory within the boundaries of the islands—as in the case of Dubai—as it is about really engaging with the systems in which the islands float. Artificial islands offer the exciting possibility of approaching landscapes as a field in which you can employ relatively small-scale platforms to transform vast territories, as opposed to actually design vastness. Perhaps the next step lies in a new wave of islands as itinerant vessels. There is already a fascinating and extensive history of floating hospitals, casinos, hotels, et cetera, but there are not enough examples of interesting itinerant and floating public spaces. The discipline of landscape architecture has not yet seen a single practice committed to floating surfaces—whether aquatic or atmospheric—in contrast to the sixties and seventies, when so many architecture practices envisioned floating buildings.

GM: Would you say that fiction is often equally important in your own work?

LC: Definitely. The first project that I built started as a fiction in a way. We were doing the competition for an aquatic center in Medellín in 2008, just four months after starting the practice, and we honestly never thought we would win that one. It had a lot of speculation in it—images of water surrounded by more water, and we decided to do a building without walls or a roof. Our entry was a serious fiction about responding to an architecture competition brief with a landscape operation. We won, and two years after that we were swimming in those pools! I experienced that just after starting the practice, and now I never question the seriousness of crafted fictions.

▲ CF. 51

fig. 1 Airport as Island (2012),
La Carlota Airport Park.
Proposal for the transformation of
Caracas's airport into a
metropolitan park

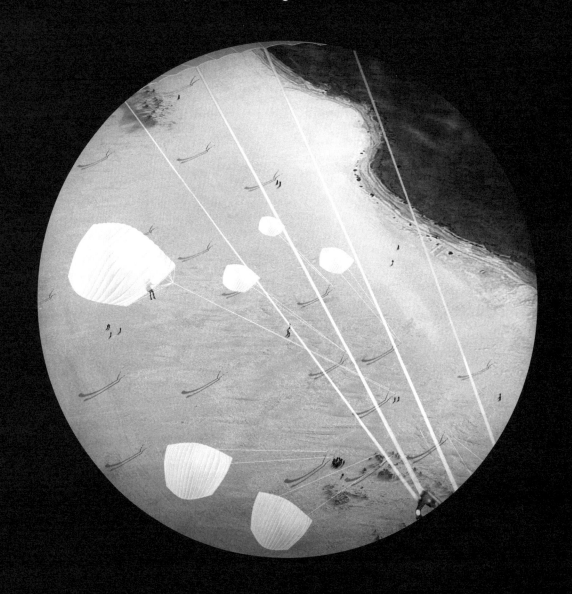

# WEATHERFIELD

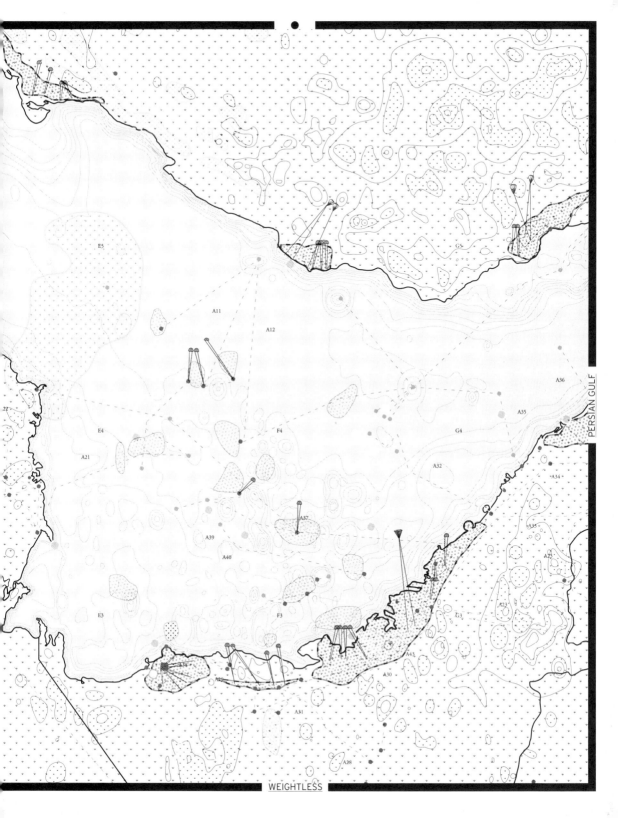

○

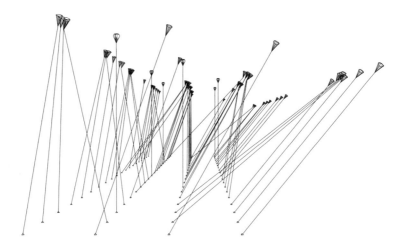

Situated along a sandy beach front in Abu Dhabi in the United Arab Emirates between the islands of Yas and Saadiyat, the project provides a public space capable of harvesting the abundant renewable resource of wind energy in the Middle East. Unlike current renewable energy fields where technologies are publicly inaccessible, static, and always on, this shape-shifting energy generation park offers a range of public engagement dependent on wind, sun, and moisture. Thus, energy generation becomes a public performance.

Organized and designed to respond efficiently and creatively to climate, the park serves as a barometer of regional weather events; it is active during weather events and calm when weather is calm, offering a compatible experience in each instance. It is simultaneously a public space, a dynamic energy icon, and a public weather service. As a registration of daily weather events such as Shamal winds, dense fog, and sandstorms, the kites use a parafoil system inflated by wind to remain aloft and a Windbelt system to harvest the "flutter" energy from the wind.

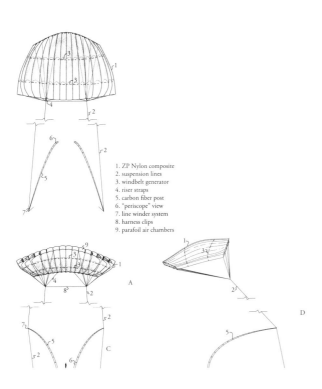

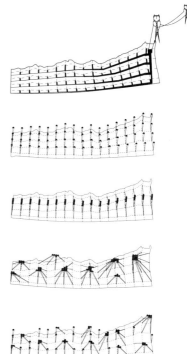

1. ZP Nylon composite
2. suspension lines
3. windbelt generator
4. riser straps
5. carbon fiber post
6. "periscope" view
7. line winder system
8. harness clips
9. parafoil air chambers

A

D

C

▲ CF. 54–55, 56–57

fig. 1 Different organizations based on diverse weather events and a link to the energy grid

fig. 2 Detail of kite prototype

× × × × × × × × × ×

fig. 3 View from the desert between Yas and Saadiyat Islands

Unlike large-scale energy infrastructures that are out-of-scale, off-site, and off-limits, the project and its energy capacity can be employed at the scale of a single-family home. The two hundred parakites would extend across the test site in a 60-meter grid. Each parakite is capable of producing 6,220 kilowatt hours of energy annually. This would culminate in 1.24 gigawatts annually across the park or about 620 energy-efficient homes. Thus, each parakite is able to power three homes for one year.

With an immense abundance of wind, there is considerable potential for the Persian Gulf to be the largest renewable energy field in the world and a model for future regional planning. Weatherfield would become a catalyst for a regional energy plan in the Middle East and an initial development phase to generate a large-scale reconsideration of energy in the entire region. This plan proposes the decommissioning of twentieth-century industrial energy fields across the Persian Gulf and their transformation into a network of twenty-first-century public energy parks.

# WELCOME TO
# FLEETWOOD

○

While the original competition brief called for a welcome sign for the city of Surrey, Canada, this project uses a floating tower to explore the expansion of the agency of a sign into a massive registration of events occurring on the Trans-Canada Highway.

The lighter-than-air tower requires structural support not for its weight but for maintaining its location. Rather than merely display a welcome sign, the Fleetwood Marker employs the benefits of tall vertical structures, such as radio transmission and observation capabilities, opening up potential

WEIGHTLESS

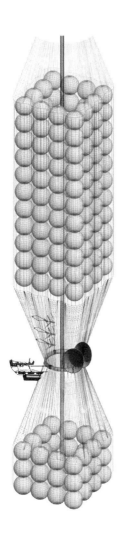

▲ **CF. 60, 61**

fig. 1 With a height of 180 meters above
street level, the tower hosts all the
communication antennas of the city.

× × × × × × × × × ×

fig. 2 Axonometric of the point
where the antennas and equipment
are fixed

fig. 3 Axonometric of the
viewing platform with
capacity for sixteen people

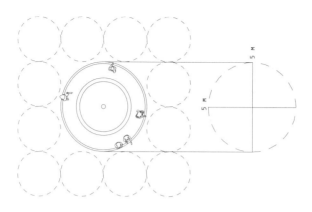

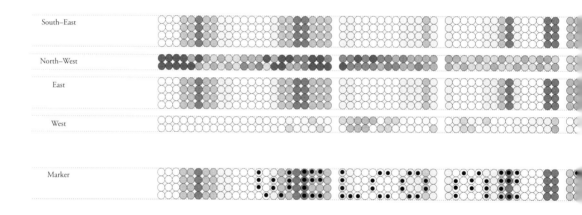

opportunities in a flat city mostly composed of low-rise buildings and bisected by a highway. Made with clusters of small weather balloons filled with helium, the tower would be the only structure in the city tall enough to facilitate communication antennas. The Fleetwood Marker also acts as a high-altitude public viewing platform, with a gondola at its base for occupation. A vertical color light show registering highway traffic is rendered on the balloon clusters and corresponds with highway activity, illuminating the installation at night.

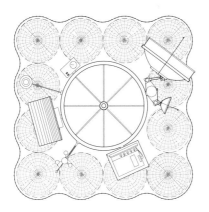

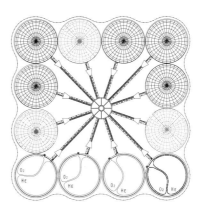

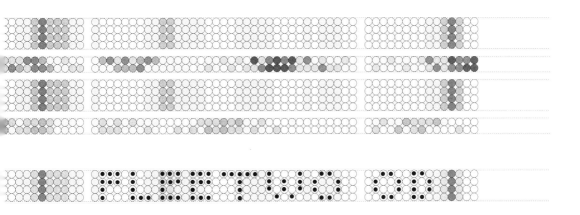

▲ CF. 62–63

figs. 4–6 Plan view of
the public platform, antennas
locations, and balloon detail

× × × × × × × × × ×

fig. 7 Elevation of the installation
displaying the welcome sign

# CLOUDS

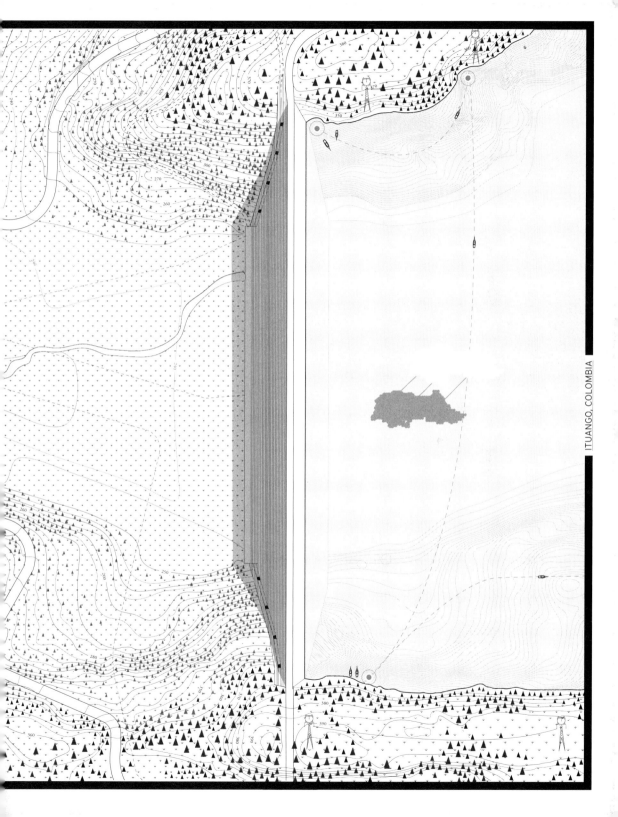

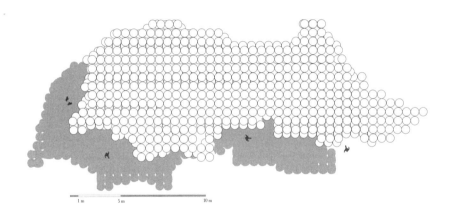

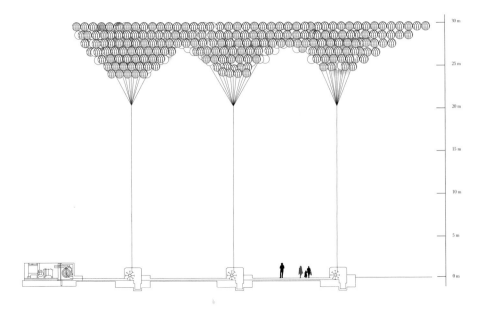

▲ CF. 66, 67

fig. 1 Section view of the installation
exposing the three electric engines
that control height. In the lowest position,
it acts as a canopy for events, while
the highest is the ideal position for
radio broadcasts.

× × × × × × × × × ×

fig. 2 Rendering of the installation in
its highest position, attached to the
Ituango hydroelectric dam

CLOUDS

▲ CF. 68–69

fig. 3 The clouds will allow for
constant broadcast of "Radio
Hidroelectrica" to towns separated
by a dramatic topography.

Projected to be the biggest
hydroelectric infrastructure in
Colombia, the proposed installation
at the Ituango hydroelectric power
plant was commissioned to generate
a physical yet temporary venue for
public awareness, discussion, and
communication of the hydroelectric
company plans.

ITUANGO, COLOMBIA

The Ituango hydroelectric power plant's public relations office commissioned the design of a high-rise totemic structure to install radio antennas necessary for the broadcast of a "hydroelectric radio." However, since the original brief did not create the necessary engagement between local residents and future events associated with the construction of the dam, the installation aimed to repurpose the commission of a high-rise totemic structure into a temporary itinerant venue. Once deployed, it would serve as a covered stage in its lower positions, while in the highest ones it would serve as a platform for radio transmission and weather prediction systems.

**AIRPLOT**

WEIGHTLESS

fig. 1 Balloons are deployed
on farm animals and existing
houses

AIRPLOT

As a strategy to stop air traffic above London Heathrow Airport in England, the project is an opportunity for an aerial intervention and demonstration. While the objective of such a barricade would be to provide the owners of small properties and farms surrounding Heathrow with a tool to stop the airport's operations for a few days, it aims to prohibit the construction of a third runway.

A "navigation easement" allows property owners or potential purchasers to waive any putative notion of air rights near an airport, for convenience in future real estate transactions as well as to avoid lawsuits from future owners who might claim distress from overflying aircraft. Yet the law recognizes that landowners have property rights in the lower reaches of the airspace above their property. In balancing the public interest in using the airspace for air navigation against the landowners's rights, the law declares that landowners own only as much of the airspace above their property as they may reasonably use in connection with their enjoyment of the underlying land. In other words, landowners cannot arbitrarily try to prevent

aircraft from flying over their land by erecting spike poles, for example. However, landowners may make any legitimate use of their property they want, even if it interferes with aircraft overflying the land. Property owners surrounding Heathrow will make a legitimate reclamation of their airspace by launching tethered inflatable copies of objects or even animals. This coordinated action responds to a competition brief that originally requested the construction of a fortification in order to stop the construction of the third runway.

▲ CF. 73

fig. 2 Diagram of inflatable copies of houses, farm animals, vehicles, and small-scale infrastructure that float around Heathrow Airport. The height and location depends on the proximity to the airfield.

○

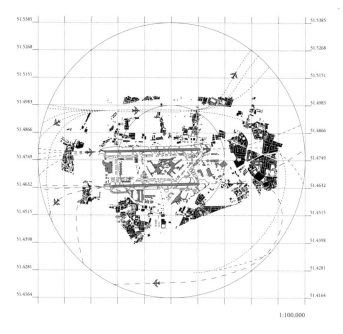

1:100,000

▲ CF. 74, 75

fig. 3 Plan of ideal location for inflatables to
maximize interference with air traffic above
Heathrow Airport

fig. 4 Axonometric view of flight path above the
airport and surrounding area

× × × × × × × × × ×

fig. 5 Model of a group of balloon copies hovering
above the real structures and animals

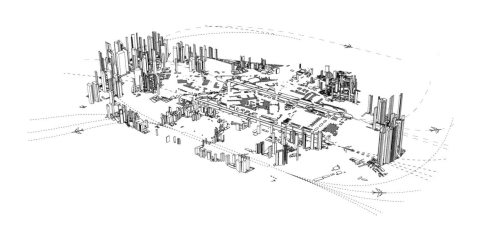

WEIGHTLESS

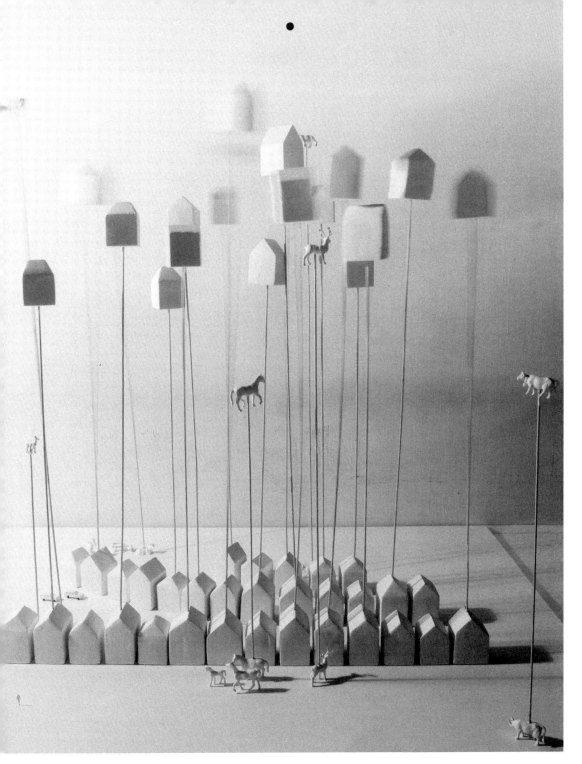

WEIGHTLESS

# Afterword

## Atmospherics: The Hydraulic Ecologies of Luis Callejas

### Charles Waldheim

▲

Charles Waldheim
is the John E. Irving
Professor and Chair
of the Department of Landscape
Architecture at the Harvard
Graduate School of Design.

The work of Luis Callejas collected here is embodied through an astonishing array of recent proposals exhibiting fluency with a range of scales and subject matter. Callejas's provocative appropriation of the culturally loaded term *landscape* to describe his practice signals an ambivalence toward the identity of the architect. It also points toward his literacy with architectural culture beyond his native Colombia and the recent recovery of landscape as a medium of design. Callejas's appropriation of landscape as a frame for a diverse body of work illustrates an appetite for addressing the ecological imperatives of contemporary design culture as well as the diverse array of international environments in which he finds his work projected. In this regard, Callejas's projects have as much to do with curating atmospheres through the hydraulics of water and air as with constructing buildings.

Callejas's interest in the aqueous and the aerial might be read in relation to contemporary debates over the critical and the performative in architecture. The work exposes a particular interest in a radically decentralized notion of site, one that is often conceived as an island, whether airborne or literally at sea. In contrast with work that eschews or denies context, Callejas's projects often radically delimit their sitedness, thereby revealing some latent, local conditions isolated from larger territorial conditions. With this deft move, Callejas distinguishes his interests from a purely instrumental environmentalism and any vestige of naive regionalism.

The projects assembled here transcend some of their more obvious precedents by pushing the limits of the architectural object up to and well beyond its limits, into environments, experiences, and atmospheres. Many fail to form into any object whatsoever. Those that do mitigate their seeming solidity by filling it with fluids that undermine any architectonic claim. These projects often invoke the aqueous, the aerial, or both. At their best, they correlate the aerial to the hydrological and suggest the need for a more general theory of hydraulics in contemporary architecture. While these effects can occasionally manifest themselves through architectural artifice or edification, they are best described through that dated term *landscape*. While much of architectural culture has been actively engaged in resisting the rise of environmental considerations as an infringement on the long-standing project of autonomy, Callejas has firmly declared his commitments to the messy and productive potentials of landscape in relation to that question. In so doing, he offers an example of genuine innovation and a whiff of the new. In locating the site for the work between effect and the phenomenal experience of atmospheric conditions, Callejas identifies a third faction between the false opposition of a strict instrumentality, on the one hand, and the project of pure autonomy, on the other.

Many of these projects depend on specific horticultural or botanical knowledge. Yet it would be a misreading of the work to accept these projects as traditional landscape architecture with a focus on plant material as a medium of design. Rather, these projects often illustrate an ambidextrous quality, equally fluent in landform and ecological processes as with architectonic language and spatial composition. What these various methodological approaches share is an interest in the specific media of atmosphere itself: water and air. In built examples, like the Aquatic Center for Medellín, underwater activities are exposed to pedestrians and the city. In that case the aquatic logic and experiential potential of water, as well as the ephemeral effects on light and air, offer the primary operating systems of a complex yet refined public realm. Farther afield, recent competition entries for the Parc del Lago in Quito, Ecuador, and the Venice Lagoon reveal an ongoing commitment to the various potentials of a hydrological urbanism. In Quito the proposal juxtaposes the reflectivity and endlessness of pools stretching to the horizon of an abandoned airfield with the reflective metallic surfaces of the airplanes that once occupied them. In contrast with the bright light and clear blue waters of Quito, the Venice Lagoon project plumbs the murky impenetrable depths of a dark, dank Venice. In both examples the particular experiential qualities of the site are revealed through the most fundamental of elements. Equally, these projects explore the associated experiential conditions of fecund humidity or luminous aridity while constructing complex public venues through the ambient and atmospheric conditions of water in its various states. In more recent projects such as the master plan for the preservation of an archipelago in the Dnieper River in Kiev, Ukraine, Callejas is more intensely committed to building complex public realms through the material and phenomenal properties of water. Ultimately, these commitments come to describe urban form as well. The line of investigation pursued by Callejas might be described by the term *atmospherics*. In pushing his architecture

to the limits of the object, beyond the question of ground, into the realm of climate and humidity, Callejas proposes a pneumatic architecture evident through the public spectacle of aerial suspension. In his proposals for monumental yet weightless structures for Heathrow Airport's guerrilla decommissioning through balloons or for the commemoration of communities affected by the Ituango hydroelectric power plant in Colombia, Callejas proposes a new age of inflatables, and a commensurate era of atmospheric affect.

Through his pursuit of projects beyond the earthly concerns of weight and mass, Callejas proposes an architecture of atmospherics. In this realm liquid water, water vapor, and ice emerge as primary representational media for new forms of public life. The fleeting experiential qualities of air and water as seen through light are orchestrated much in the way that the sequential experience of space was orchestrated by the typologies and subjectivities of landscape architecture. In pursuing the ends of architecture, Luis Callejas's projects transcend the limits of the architectural object while renewing the cultural potential of architecture as a medium of individual experience and collective public life. While this body of work is still nascent, the energy, ambition, and optimism of these projects suggest that an architecture of atmospherics may very well be an important way of thinking through contemporary design culture across disciplines.

ACKNOWLEDGMENTS

▲

To Silvia Mujica
Mariana Callejas
Rodrigo Callejas

I worked with Edgar Mazo and Sebastian Mejia under the name of Paisajes Emergentes until 2011. They are the most influential friends and architects I've come across. The following projects were authored in Medellín with Paisajes Emergentes: Venice Lagoon (20–25), Rio Olympic Park (26–31), Lake Park (32–39), Floodings (44–49), Weatherfield (52–57), Clouds (64–69), and Aquatic Center (78).

The following project was authored in association with Lateral Office (Lola Shepard and Mason White) in 2009: Weatherfield (52–57).

The following project was authored in São Paulo, Brazil, in association with Grupo SP, Una Arquitetos, and Republica Arquitetura in 2011: Rio Olympic Park (26–31).

The following projects were authored with Melissa Naranjo between 2011 and 2013, who joined me in shaping a new form of operation after Paisajes Emergentes's dissolution: Reclaiming an Archipelago (4–7), Tactical Archipelago (8–19), Rio Olympic Park (26–31), and La Carlota Airport Park (51).

The following project was authored in association with Juan Pablo Martinez: Venice Lagoon (20–25).

The following project was authored in association with Anita Berrizbeitia, Felipe Correa, Danilo Martic, Elias Gonzales, Pablo Perez Ramos, and Mariuz Klemenz: La Carlota Airport Park (51).

The following people collaborated on the projects featured in this book: Clara Arango, Juan Esteban Gomez, Sara Helgreen, Alexander Laing, Lovisa Lindstrom, Victor Marechal, Erica Martinez, Farid Maya, Manon Mollard, Sebastian Monsalve, Catalina Patiño, Lukas Pauer, Luis Tobon, Manuel Villa, and Tess Walraven.

The illustrations on the framed pages were drawn by Melissa Naranjo of LCLA Office.

The photographs on p44 and p78 were taken by Alexander Laing.

Thanks to Lukas Pauer and Melissa Naranjo for their role as assistant editors within LCLA Office.

Thanks to Carolyn Deuschle, Geoff Manaugh, Jacob Moore, Camilo Restrepo, and Mason White for their feedback on this publication.

The dialogues and support with the following have been influential and insightful: Anita Berrizbeitia, Mariana Callejas, Rodrigo Callejas, Alexander Laing, Janike Kampevold Larsen, Edgar Mazo, Sebastian Mejia, Felipe Mesa, Miguel Mesa, Silvia Mujica, Melissa Naranjo, Lukas Pauer, Catalina Patiño, Camilo Restrepo, Manuel Villa, Charles Waldheim, and Antonio Yemail

The following institutions have played a key role as platforms for discussion of the ideas presented in this book: Harvard University, University of Toronto, Universidad Nacional de Colombia, Universidad Pontificia Bolivariana, Oslo School of Architecture and Design, and Archipiélago de Arquitectura

Pamphlet Architecture was initiated in 1977 as an independent vehicle to criticize, question, and exchange views. Each issue is assembled by an individual author/architect.

For information, Pamphlet proposals, or contributions, please write to: Pamphlet Architecture, c/o Princeton Architectural Press, 37 East Seventh Street, New York, NY 10003, or go to pamphletarchitecture.org

Pamphlets published:

1. *Bridges*,
S. Holl, 1977*

2. *10 California Houses*,
M. Mack, 1978*

3. *Villa Prima Facie*,
L. Lerup, 1978*

4. *Stairwells*,
L. Dimitriu, 1979*

5. *Alphabetical City*,
S. Holl, 1980

6. *Einstein Tomb*,
L. Woods, 1980*

7. *Bridge of Houses*,
S. Holl, 1981*

8. *Planetary Architecture*,
Z. Hadid, 1981*

9. *Rural and Urban House Types*, S. Holl, 1981*

10. *Metafisica della Architettura*,
A. Sartoris, 1984*

11. *Hybrid Buildings*,
J. Fenton, 1985

12. B*uilding; Machines*,
R. McCarter, 1987

13. *Edge of a City*,
S. Holl, 1991

14. *Mosquitoes*,
K. Kaplan, T. Krueger, 1993

15. *War and Architecture*,
L. Woods, 1993

16. *Architecture as a Translation of Music*, E. Martin, 1994

17. *Small Buildings*,
M. Caldwell, 1996

19. *Reading Drawing Building*,
M. Silver, 1996

20. *Seven Partly Underground Rooms*,
M. A. Ray, 1997

21. *Situation Normal...*,
Lewis.Tsurumaki.Lewis, 1998

22. *Other Plans*,
Michael Sorkin Studio, 2001

23. *Move*,
J. S. Dickson, 2002

24. *Some Among Them Are Killers*,
D. Ross, 2003

25. *Gravity*,
J. Cathcart et al., 2003

26. *13 Projects for the Sheridan Expressway*, J. Solomon, 2004

27. *Tooling*,
Aranda/Lasch, 2006

28. *Augmented Landscapes*,
Smout Allen, 2007

29. *Ambiguous Spaces*,
Naja & deOstos, 2008

30. *Coupling*,
InfraNet Lab / Lateral Office, 2010

31. *New Haiti Villages*,
S. Holl, 2011

32. *Resilience*,
Stasus, 2012

*out of print, available only in the collection *Pamphlet Architecture 1–10.*